Advance Praise

"If you are ready to step into your authentic feminine power and become the woman you were meant to be, this essential book will provide a much needed light along the way."

~ Laura Davis, bestselling author of *The Courage to Heal* and *I Thought We'd Never Speak Again*

"In a world, where women are often expected to become "better men" in order to succeed in business and life, it is easy to forget our powerful feminine essence. Vanessa shows us how to rediscover our inner feminine power and to remain true to ourselves, while navigating our daily challenges. This is great for us adults and especially valuable for our young girls who need strong and feminine women as healthy role models!"

~ Bettina Gordon, International Journalist and Conscious Living Expert

"*The 5 Feminine Power Virtues* is written with so much love and devotion for women. While reading through this work of love I became very aware of the essence of my femininity, something I had somehow neglected. Vanessa speaks to your soul and gives your mind the tools to re-connect with our feminine virtues. Every woman and young girl need to read this book!"

~ Ada Novak, Founder of Laya Center, A Sanctuary for Women

Advance Praise

"Brilliant! This book takes you on a journey into the feminine where you emerge as a powerful visionary leader who accesses her true power from within. This is a cutting edge book that defines freedom, fulfillment, and joy from a feminine model."

~ Suzy Manning, CEO of SIZZZL, Powerful Women Who Ignite the World

"By Vanessa opening her heart so willingly with her own experiences, she enables other women to easily follow suit and begin to live a life encompassing the five feminine virtues for ultimate happiness."

~ Angela Dacey, Colour Strategist and Personal Development Expert

"I loved the way Vanessa wrote about what in essence every woman should remember and practice in her life, so simple and yet so profound."

~ Valeria Grunbaum, International Speaker, Trainer, Coach & Author of *Success with International Customers*

The 5 Feminine Power Virtues

A Woman's Spiritual Roadmap
to Love, Joy & Fulfillment

By Vanessa Halloum

THE 5 FEMININE POWER VIRTUES
A Woman's Spiritual Roadmap to Love, Joy & Fulfillment

Published by: **Empowered Life Productions**
P.O. Box 670513, Coral Springs, FL 33067
www.EmpoweredLifeProductions.com
954-543-0434

ISBN 978-0-9854983-0-6 (paperback)
Library of Congress Control Number: 2012937560

Cover Artwork by Mihaela Grozdanova
Author Photograph: © Marilyn Garcia

Dedication

To 5 Feminine Souls Who Changed My Life:

My mother…Solange
My sister…Aline
My goddaughter…Priscilla
My niece…Erika
My grandmother…Vó Maria

You have all touched me deeply and
inspired me to follow my path.

Table of Contents

Introduction

"She's a powerful woman."

What comes to mind when you read those words? Do you envision a wealthy, well-dressed woman who commands attention? Does she run a highly successful company and maintain a perfect home life? Maybe she is physically capable and strong?

For me, a powerful woman possesses emotional strength and has the courage to be herself, no matter what the circumstance. I envision a deeply feminine woman who lives life on her own terms. She creates her life, like an artist painting a masterpiece. This woman has internal power—the most priceless kind of all.

But it's not always easy to tap into our natural, feminine strength. As women, we've been trained to give our power away in this world dominated by masculinity. We quiet ourselves when we want to shout. We apologize instead of express. We adhere to social rules that stifle and mute our true selves. When we do reach for power, we often model our pursuit after men and their approach.

And while we may obtain success by using this masculine model, it's not sustainable because it doesn't provide us with what we really need. The truth is, we don't have to fight and compete like men to be empowered. We are the most powerful when we step fully into our feminine selves

The Power of Doing and Being

There are two kinds of power: doing and being. Most of us relate power with action (doing). This is the domain we often associate with men. It's a hierarchical type of command we've seen repeatedly in society.

This is not the type of power we will be talking about in this book. We will address the "being" kind of power, more closely associated with women. We will rediscover the unbridled strength of feminine essence once again—full, passionate, and authentic—because deep inside we know that true power transcends the external world.

This book will take you on a highly personal journey where you will reacquaint yourself with *The 5 Feminine Power Virtues*: Presence, Authenticity, Sensuality, Spirituality and Gratitude. Of course, the virtues discussed in this book are no secret; they are ideals that form our daily existence to some degree. But the secret lies in the *strength* behind these virtues, which is often left untapped and ignored.

Each short chapter will explain the relevance of these virtues in your life and how they can shape a new way of existing in today's world. I will also offer exercises so you can hone and practice these virtues in your own time.

You'll notice a certain simplicity in approach to these virtues; this is not some complicated, heady philosophy. As women, we inherently know the benefits of feminine ideals, but we've lost touch with them. They are waiting to offer us guidance, strength, passion of purpose and a better overall sense of well-being.

You are sitting on a gold mine—and that gold mine is *you*.

For Women Only

This book is specifically for women because we operate differently. We can't expect to live a fulfilling life by following in the footsteps of men and using the same tools they do. That's like giving an electrician the tools a carpenter uses to do his (or her) job.

The virtues examined in this book are dedicated to women. Of course, men can cultivate these virtues as well. Men have a feminine side, just as women possess masculine traits. Unfortunately, for both women and men, that feminine side has gone underground. It's time to revive those aspects of ourselves and come back to life again, on our terms.

As women, we are leading much more stressful lives and have a wide array of personal and professional demands pressing upon us. It's easy to get overwhelmed and burned out. The dangers of our "on the go" lifestyle are obvious: health problems, addiction issues, eating disorders...the list goes on. Yet we still trudge forward, like dutiful zombies, living a seemingly full life that secretly tires and depletes us.

This book serves as a gentle guide, intended to reconnect you with your deepest feminine essence. You will learn to draw from that essence like an ever-flowing fountain. You will feel whole again. Many of us, at one time or another, have abandoned these potent aspects of our womanhood—myself included—thinking that it was a sign of weakness. Nothing could be further from the truth. Our power lies dormant within our femininity. If we have the courage to dig deep inside and experience our feminine essence in an authentic way, we will discover a power we never imagined.

There's a spiritual imperative at hand. We *need* to find that balance between our masculine and feminine energies now. By reconnecting with these key virtues, you will choose life, health and wholeness once again. You'll begin to feel a vibrancy long forgotten.

The best part? These virtues require less doing and more being.

And you've already taken the first step.

Enjoy the journey!

CHAPTER 1
Living in Presence

The miracle of love comes to you in the presence of the uninterrupted moment. If you are mentally somewhere else, you miss real life.

~ Byron Katie

What Is Presence?

Presence is awareness. Presence is being here now. Presence is living fully in the moment, without being distracted by nagging thoughts ricocheting inside your head.

Presence has become an overlooked state of mind in the last few decades. In our society, we pride ourselves in our ability to multi-task. Hundreds of things compete for our attention:

emails, deadlines, appointments, phone calls, text messages...the list goes on. Often, we're in the middle of one task and already planning for the next. We've become so accustomed to this frenetic lifestyle that distraction is considered normal. Peace of mind is passé.

But whenever we have the rare opportunity to meet someone who truly embodies the quality of presence, they stand out completely. We can feel the difference tangibly, and secretly, we breathe a sigh of relief. Ah...*this* is what it feels like to be living life, not racing through it. This is what it feels like to live, rather than worry about life.

Perhaps you've had the good fortune to meet this type of person. When he or she walks into a room, everyone notices. Something within them calls our attention. It's palpable and we are immediately attracted to it. It awakens something in all of us. This is the outward manifestation of presence.

People living in the present are totally conscious of the here and now with no judgments or preconceived notions of the way things should be. They are not thinking about the errands they need to run, what they're going to make for dinner or what people might be saying about them. These people seem unique but the truth is that presence is our natural state of being. We just lose our way when we get caught up in busyness, doing and preoccupation.

When we become too anxious, self-conscious or busy orchestrating every detail of our life, we are no longer present. Compare it to a first date, where we're so focused on saying and doing just the right thing that we lose the ability to simply enjoy meeting a new person. We become "stuck in our heads."

On the other hand, when we make passionate love to someone we care about or are consumed by a creative endeavor, we completely let go and surrender to the moment. We become one with our life and who we are.

But these pure, blissful and present moments are often few and far between. Most of us allow our egos to take over. We're often *in reaction* to the world around us, which implies a certain defensiveness. Creativity decreases, calm is replaced by anxiety. The ego is now in charge, playing different games and roles, always thinking it's not good enough or that we're better than someone else.

Why do we let our egos run the show? Because we're trained to think there's something better off in the distance. Our "perfect" life awaits somewhere but certainly not in the here and now. Promises of a better future await, so we perpetually chase after it like a rabbit on the run. Problem is, we never seem to arrive at our destination. We remain locked in a perpetual state of need for that elusive "something else."

The truth is that you don't need anything else. You could stop reading this book right now and transform your entire life if you simply focused on being more present in your life. This, unfortunately, is easier said than done. (But you knew that, right?)

Shifting Focus from There to Here

So how do we break this perpetual cycle of focusing on the past or the future? How do we become reacquainted with the present? Awareness and redirection are key. Most of us are aware of that old rubber band trick, where you snap a band around your wrist when a craving or unwanted thought surfaces. The sting of the rubber band against your skin breaks the habitual pattern and breaks you out of the trance. You become conscious of the rut you were stuck in and are able to make a different choice. It's a simple but very effective tool.

Imagine a mental rubber band, which you consciously snap whenever you start becoming anxious about a future event or buried in an old story from your past. It's that kind of immediate awareness—that snap—that breaks the old, stale mental habit and brings you immediately into the present. (Feel free to wear an actual rubber band if that helps!)

After all, the present moment is all we really have. The past will never be anything more than a memory. And the future, well....anything could happen. So why waste time on the complete unknown? Perhaps because we feel the need to control it so nothing bad happens. But we all know that's impossible. Besides, would you want to control every moment in your life? Where is the mystery in that?

Put it this way: think of the most pivotal moments in your life. Did you see them coming? Did you wake up knowing you'd get in that car accident? Did you know a week beforehand that you'd be laid off from your job? Were you aware that you'd be proposed to by the man you love? No, probably not. Life is a series of curve balls. We can prepare all we want, but in the end, we can never predict it all. Releasing the need to control the future is a relief, ultimately. It's a tense grip on the ungraspable. It's a waste of energy!

Of course, there are many positive ways to be present and envision your future by setting intentions, just as there are ways to examine your past in a thoughtful and therapeutic manner. As a matter of fact, real change only occurs when we're present and able to set intentions or heal old pains. But it must be from a place of awareness, not one of submersion in worry, obsession or grief.

Presence in Everyday Practice

Being present applies to every aspect of our lives; whether we are playing tennis, giving a presentation at work, cooking a gourmet meal, driving a car, eating, crying, or laughing, presence can empower and strengthen us. We all know how much trouble distraction can cause (texting while driving for instance). Just imagine the possibilities for connection, creativity and joy when you are fully present.

Athletes practice for countless hours, yet when they compete, they let go of their preconceived notions and training, becoming completely present in competition. This is called "being in the zone."

If you're a golfer and you think too much about the swing, it becomes too mechanical or forced and doesn't work. When you're present, there's no physical stress because there's no real sense of physical strain—there's only flow.

So why isn't presence practiced every day in all aspects of our world?

Because most of us are used to living in our heads, where inner dialogues play constantly, usually mired in negativity. Meanwhile life is happening right before us. Yet we're stuck in our "stories." Our stories, unfortunately, aren't even all that accurate, but we believe them wholeheartedly at the moment. We don't realize how tainted they are by insecurities, fears and anxiety.

These stories are often deeply embedded and are not of the happy variety either. They're usually packed with resentment, resistance and complaints. When was the last time you played out an argument in your head? "I should have said X to Y then Z would have happened." You play it again and again, but the story itself never really changes.

As Eckhart Tolle says in his amazing book, *A New Earth*:

> *When you hate what you are doing, complain about your surroundings, curse things that are happening or have happened, or when your internal dialogue consists of should and shouldn'ts, of blaming and accusing, then you are arguing with what is, arguing with that which is always already the case. You are making Life into an enemy and Life says, 'War is what you want, and war is what you get.' External reality, which always reflects back to you your inner state, is then experienced as hostile.*

There is no real presence without complete and total acceptance of the here and now. So much of life is spent rejecting our current situation, and at times, we feel desperate to change it. Of course, there's nothing wrong with wanting to change aspects of our lives, but if we refuse to accept the way things are first, we're denying ourselves all of the wonders of life now.

My own path in finding true presence was met with a considerable amount of internal fear at first. If I simply let go and accepted my life as is, would I ever be able to make real changes in my life? Maybe I would become lazy or complacent. Maybe my dreams would never become realized. Luckily, just the opposite is true.

I remember a time when I had worked so hard to get the job of my dreams. I finally had "made it." I had a fancy title, a handsome paycheck and rewarding work. I had manifested everything I wanted. But I had forgotten to ask for one thing: a nice boss—or at least someone I could work with easily enough. This boss was *mean*—not just to me but to everyone I worked with. And worse, she was the kind of person who knew how to put on a fake smile when needed, so she seemed perfectly likable to the outside world. You know the type, right?

My boss persistently placed more and more unnecessary pressures on my colleagues and me. After a few months, I was miserable and under so much stress that I gained 30 pounds. I would come home from work and cry for hours. If it weren't for the fact that I loved everything else about my job, I probably would have left. Instead, I put up with it for eight long months. It took me that amount of time to realize I already had everything I needed to turn the situation around.

I started experimenting with acceptance, simply letting things be just the way they were. It was a monumental effort at first, but it became easier with time. I used every tool I could find to help me: journaling, books, audiobooks, affirmations, meditation—you name it, I tried it. I remember listening to Rick Jarow's audiobook, *The Yoga of Work*, and being intrigued by the concept that we need to do less in order to find the job or career we were meant to have.

Rick Jarow addresses the fact that most of us choose jobs simply because of the amount of money we are going to make, not because of the amount of joy we are going to feel. Once we begin to shift our consciousness and become more present to what's going on in front of us, including how we're feeling and what we need to be happy, there's less of a need to do anything per se. We become more observant of the moment. We see things we hadn't noticed before, things we overlooked because of our busyness. An inner knowing will arise and our actions appear spontaneously, not because we think we need to do anything, but because something inside of us is guiding us.

At first, I thought that was a crazy idea, but I decided to give it a try. Heck, I had nothing to lose. The most amazing thing happened—it worked!

I simply set the intention that I wanted to find a workplace where I would feel comfortable, work with people that I liked and who appreciated my work, while simultaneously accepting my current situation.

Within a month, the HR department at a company where a friend of mine worked found me on the Internet and by "coincidence" asked my friend's opinion on my qualifications. My friend not only exclaimed that she knew me but informed her that I might be leaving my current position. About five weeks later, I was working at a job with less stress, better pay, co-workers I could relate to, and a boss that truly appreciated me.

The Universe works in mysterious ways and we might not always understand how it all plays out—and we don't need to. All we need to do is be in acceptance of what's going on *now*. If we decide that it's not something we want, that's okay, but we need to remain in acceptance of it, as a first step. (What you resist persists anyway.)

When you approach your life with open arms, you're in a more positive state of mind where real change can occur.

Conversely, when you're in a bad mood, it's almost as if you attract accidents, arguments and roadblocks. When you accept the present for what it is, you have a surplus of energy to create change in your life.

That's because living from the present shifts your focus entirely. You're no longer swimming upstream. Change occurs more naturally and you become more aware of opportunities when they arrive. Presence is a subtle shift that gives you immense inner power to create the life of your dreams—without all the worry and struggle!

Why Is Presence So Important For Women?

The feminine movement is experiencing many exciting changes right now. We are gaining power back on our terms. It's exciting to witness so many women unabashedly going after their dreams. It's our time as women to let our true selves shine and make a huge impact on the planet. And we're going to expand even further!

But with power comes responsibility. As we awaken to our true inner power, we need to access the right tools and resources that allow us to grow safely and sanely.

Being present is one of the tools we need to stay extremely aware of the world around us. We can't allow our egos, fears or insecurities to dictate our choices. We need to stay centered and focused to enact long-standing change. It's a new paradigm of feminine existence.

Feminine energy has been suppressed for a long time. If we are to fulfill our destinies, we need to forgive the past and create a new future by living fully and completely in the present. We have been living in a world with a serious imbalance of masculine energy and we are ready to bring balance and harmony back into our lives and the world in which we live.

But it all starts with the need to be present and aware—of our emotional state, our health, our relationships, danger, opportunities...the list goes on.

Presence in Relationships

Relationships often end because neither party is fully present; neither person is relating to the other in an active, engaging way. They talk, but it feels empty and both partners feel alone. Constant "life distractions" create a chasm and disconnect. (We've all seen the couple at a restaurant, seemingly more married to their cell phones than one another!)

As women, we have the power to fortify any relationship when we bring that sense of emotional presence into our relationships. Women are sensitive beings and are often more naturally connected with their inner world.

By bringing these qualities into a difficult interpersonal situation, you will be able to make a huge impact and create change without necessarily having to say or do anything. Your present, emotional being is what will initiate the change in your partner, or better yet, awaken something in your partner that will bring more love and light into your relationship.

How? Because being present is like shining a powerful light in a dark room. It guides the way when you and a loved one are feeling lost. If you're not getting locked into an old story, it makes it hard for your partner to do the same. You lead by example, by being emotionally "there and aware." Communication becomes more accessible and easier.

Deciding To Be Present

When something is meaningful to you, you immediately become more present. If someone is relaying life-changing events to you, you want to hear it completely. You are present.

If you see a moving performance, you are there, fully and completely. Meaning is cultivated by presence.

Often when we say, "I'm not feeling it," we simply aren't diving into the moment. We're dragging our feet in the past or worrying about the future. We're energetically bogged down. We're not in tune with our emotional states or our current situations.

So how do you become more engaged and "feel it" more frequently? It's simply a decision you need to make—hit the "stop" button on that tired old tape and shift your focus 100% to the moment at hand.

A good practice is to become more aware of your thoughts and remind yourself that you don't always need to buy into them. Start questioning them. They're only thoughts, after all. Just like moods and passing clouds, they change constantly.

Many people allow their thoughts and inner dialogue to run wild inside of their heads. Our goal is to transcend thought. We do this by realizing we are not our thoughts; we are the consciousness *behind* our thoughts. Remember: unhappiness doesn't come from any situation or circumstance; it comes from our thoughts surrounding the situation.

The present, on the other hand, is neutral and beautiful *as is*. Focus on the facts instead of the stories your mind creates about the present. Become the awareness behind your thoughts.

How to Increase Your Emotional Awareness

Simply deciding to be more present in your life is the first step. Your mind recognizes these choices. Your subconscious takes them in and begins assimilating more presence into your existence.

The next step is a more conscious one: become more engaged in what you are doing. Develop more passion for the moment. Go back to that rubber band technique; when you feel you are slipping into worry or upset or distraction mode, snap that mental band. Take in the world around you. What does it look like? Feel like? Smell like? What small details do you notice? How are you feeling?

Be completely open and receptive to your emotional state. But be aware: there's a difference between being overly emotional and being in touch with your emotions. Emotions are completely natural and we feel them all of the time, whether we are aware of them or not. Getting in touch with them reminds us of how we're feeling now; it naturally increases our sense of presence. Maybe you need a good cry, for example. Or a loving hug from a friend. Or social engagement.

Being overly emotional means being ruled by your emotional state, not in touch with it. Those old stories—and our repetitive emotional baggage—are playing full blast in our heads, and we're far from being present.

Our emotions are not good or bad—they simply are, like the weather. They serve to awaken something inside of us or shine the light on an issue we might need to tend to. They are not who we are and they don't define us. They are indicators, road signs.

If we attach too much importance to our emotions, they begin to run the show. We become prisoners to them. On the flip side, being too detached from your emotional state results in a type of emotional numbness. We disconnect too much and walk around like zombies.

Use your emotions to your advantage; don't let them use you.

Steps to Living in a State of Presence

Here are a few exercises that will help you cultivate more awareness and presence in your life:

- ***Practice creating meaningful moments in your life.*** For example, when someone you love comes in the room, make a choice to be completely present by giving them 100% of your attention. Look at them in the eye and give them a big smile.

- ***Start thinking of ways you can create magical moments in your life.*** Often a walk outdoors is the first step. Magic abounds in nature.

- ***Close your eyes and become completely present.*** Start moving your body very slowly and gently, feeling entirely conscious of each movement, each breath. Dance with presence in mind.

- ***Practice active listening.*** Most of us are not good listeners, even if we think we are. Don't wait for a pause so you can speak. Be completely present to what the other person's saying, even if you don't get a chance to respond.

- ***During any moment of the day, ask yourself:*** "What am I focusing on and making a priority: the past, present or the future?" Pay attention to the answer that comes up most frequently when you ask yourself this question. If it's the past or the future, then you'll know that you have more work to do.

- ***Bring conscious actions and movement to your everyday activities,*** even if for only a few minutes at a time. Presence increases with practice, so small amounts of time really make a long-lasting difference.

- ***Be aware of your breath throughout the day.*** Are you breathing from your chest or your belly? Try to bring your breath down to your belly and breathe consciously for at least five minutes a day.

Inner Reflections

As we begin our journey towards empowerment, it's important for us to start identifying where we are creating stories and private dramas, and where we are already succeeding at being present:

- When was a time in your life when you felt totally present and passionate?

- In your daily life, when do you feel the most present? The least present?

- In what areas of your life do you tend to create a lot of drama? If you're not sure, try to remember a time when you created a whole story in your head and then realized that none of it was true.

- What stories are playing in your head right now?

- What is your current relationship with the present?

- What are you rejecting in your life by not being present?

- Who are the people in your life with whom you need to create more meaningful moments? What can you do to make more meaningful moments with them?

My Insights

Write down any thoughts and feelings that might have come up for you while reading this chapter.

Go to www.PowerVirtues.com/Presence to continue your journey of *Living in Presence*.

CHAPTER 2
Embracing Authenticity

With courage, commitment and intention, we can become our true selves: authentic, heart-centered women, light-bearers in our beleaguered world.

~ Sue Patton Thoelle, *The Courage to be Yourself*

What Is Authenticity?

Authenticity. It's such a weighted word, isn't it? You can't quite put your finger on it, but you know when you feel it. The definition of authenticity points to the most basic of principles: being yourself. Sounds like a simple concept...but what a complex and intricate journey it can be!

We know what it's like when we aren't living authentically, right? Our soul withers away a little each day, whether it's because of a job we don't like or a relationship that just isn't working out. Who we are deep inside and what we do in the world is not congruent. We feel disconnected, uneasy.

Renowned movie producer Tom Shadyac said: "*Authenticity means to be the author of your own life.*" So true. It's about creating your own story the way you envision it, instead of the way other people have told it to you. And then living it.

Authenticity is the art of knowing who you really are and fully inhabiting that wonderful being that is you. It's an art because it's a unique, creative experience for each one of us.

Authenticity is a homecoming of the soul. An awakening. A rebirth of our original state. It's an ever-evolving process, and one you can start now. You *are* that work in progress.

What "Self" Are You?

Imagine standing before a canvas. You close your eyes and see the most amazing picture in your mind's eye—one that encapsulates all the wonder and beauty you could dream. Upon opening your eyes, you need to translate that amazing vision onto the canvas. It may take a lifetime, but you're determined to create that masterpiece. That internal vision is your true, authentic self.

Many of us have created this internal vision based on someone else's story, one created by our family, our partner or society as a whole. We live in a trance, believing that's who we should be, or even who we want to be. Soon, that inner masterpiece of ours is dusty and forgotten. We've become part of someone else's masterpiece instead. And while that canvas may be beautiful, something always feels amiss.

There's a common psychological theory that there are four versions of yourself: who you think you are, who others think you are, who you think others think you are, and then lastly, who you really are. The latter is that authentic self we want to uncover; it's the version that carries no expectations or interpretations from other people. The others are all illusions.

Unfortunately, it's not always clear which version is which. That's how our journey to authenticity begins. Like spiritual archaeologists, we must dig deep inside ourselves and strip away all that excess baggage: the stories, the roles and the masks that we mistake for our authentic self. Once they are removed, we are left with nothing but our essential being. We are, once again, back to self.

But of course, removing life's baggage is no easy task! For some, it may take a lifetime. In addition, there are always *new* external expectations affecting our search for self, telling us we should be this way or that. These expectations weigh upon us and our journey is slowed down. We can easily forget who we *really* are and slip back into a trance-like state. So how can we genuinely wake up?

The Rocky Path to Authenticity

Returning to authenticity is not for the meek at heart; it takes a great deal of courage to be yourself and to show your true colors. People might reject this "true you" at first, leaving you feeling frustrated and alone. Some may shame or ridicule you. Others may feel betrayed by your changes or reject you.

I'm reminded of an incident with an ex-business partner not so long ago. I entered into a partnership that turned sour quickly. After a few months of working together, I quickly realized that it was not going to work. As I tried to end the partnership peacefully, he became more aggressive toward me. He sent threatening emails and text messages and tried to bully me into giving the business away to him.

His toxic nature was so unpleasant that I decided I would walk away and give him whatever he wanted for my peace of mind. I could no longer afford to be contaminated by his negative energy, so I hired a negotiator to deal with him directly and handle any remaining business. To my amazement, even the negotiator was unable to deal with him and when *their* communication broke down, my ex-partner's harassments and insults escalated and became personal.

During this time, I did a radio interview where I talked about living an authentic life. The next day, I received another insulting message from my ex-partner, this time proclaiming how fake I was to dare talk about authenticity.

It was so ironic. I had been dealing with an unpleasant situation by making a conscious decision to remain in my feminine essence, to stay calm and not allow this man's negativity to sap and drain my energy. In reality, I had never been so truthful to my being and my nature, yet here he was, accusing me of being inauthentic in an incredibly aggressive way!

In short, the search for authenticity can be a lonely and challenging one at times. It can inspire anger and resistance in others, as it happened with my ex-partner. But it's like a spiritual spring cleaning, which eventually feels liberating and right. The wrong people and situations, those that are incompatible with our true selves, will fall by the wayside.

For those who remain in your circle, your authenticity resonates—they get it! People close to you may even be inspired by your new path and search for their own divine inner self. You will also begin to attract new people who are more natural fits with the real you.

Why Is Authenticity Particularly Important For Women?

As women, we often focus on fulfilling other people's needs. But when we give to others first, we're left feeling unfulfilled, stressed and resentful. It's imperative to take care of ourselves before showing up for the people in our lives. Remember what you are taught during airplane safety instructions: you need to put the oxygen mask on yourself first in order to place it on others.

We are also exceedingly busy acting out roles dictated to us by society or family. We often shape our entire existence based on what we've been told. Many have long forgotten about that quiet voice that's been speaking to us the whole time.

And sometimes that voice is literal.

I'm reminded of a shy, mature woman I saw at a talent show once. She expressed to the judges and the audience that her passion had always been singing but her parents had told her she wasn't good enough.

No one was expecting much from her, as she got ready to start singing. But as she waited for the music to begin, there was a radical change in her stance and energy—a dramatic shift that seemed to be coming from a deep part of her spirit.

When she started singing, everyone was stunned. She was incredible! There wasn't a dry eye in the theater. Watching this beautiful soul finally come out of her shell reminded me that we can't allow our dreams to die because of what others say.

In this particular case, the power of someone else's negative opinion had been enough to sway the entirety of her life up until that point. And we all know the feeling. When we absorb someone else's opinions of us, we begin what I call the "comparison conflict." We are instantly off our path and only define ourselves in relation to another.

Comparing ourselves to others is a dead-end street. If you look hard enough, you will always find someone "better" or "worse" than you in just about any area of life. But life is not about being better than others; it's about becoming better than who you once were. When you challenge yourself to become more authentic, and you do so with kindness and self-love, you will grow, in relation only to yourself.

The search for authenticity in women is critical, since we have been bombarded for generations with strict (and often conflicting) messages about who we are and who we should be. We need to be smart, but not too smart. Nurturing, but suddenly sexy when required. An aggressive go-getter, but a sweet and well-mannered lady in an instant. The roles are constantly changing. We desperately try to keep up with all of them.

As I was growing up, my mother always told me to study and work hard so I would never have to depend on a man, even though that was her situation. I valued her lessons and understood why she did not want us to follow in her footsteps.

But what really confused my teenage brain was the fact that my sister and I were always the ones summoned to do any sort of housework while my brother was not expected to lift a finger, not even to pick up the clothes he'd leave lying on the bathroom floor!

On one hand, I understood that she was simply acting out of habit, but on the other hand, I was utterly frustrated. Was I supposed to work hard and be independent but remain in servitude to men as well? And certainly our family was not alone; I have witnessed countless families that live in such a conflicted fashion. It's not uncommon to meet a woman that has a full-time job but still has to do all the house chores when she comes home.

Change is not always easy, especially when we become accustomed to these varied and often conflicting roles we play. It starts when we realize we don't like the way things are going and begin to take small steps to get where we want.

It also starts when we let go of the roles we've been given by others or have put upon ourselves. We are much more than we know. As soon as we open ourselves to new possibilities and let go of expectations, we begin to create a new vision for our life.

The Three Roads To "Have It All"

Some of us have bought into the concept that we "want it all." But is that really possible? Or even at all that desirable? Great marriage, adoring kids, successful career, beautiful home, perfect social life—sounds great...but a lot of work, right? What is it you *really* want? What does the essential you really need in order to thrive?

Here are the three variations to having it all. You may recognize yourself in one category or a little bit in all:

1. ***The "I Want it All, and I'll Do What It Takes to Keep It"* Woman.** These women work hard to improve and maintain their lives. And if having it all is an option, then they want as

much as possible. They then discover that having everything isn't all it's cracked up to be. Women often suffer from burnout as they juggle a career, family, marriage, children, etc. Mental and physical problems can develop: migraines, chronic fatigue, etc. Often these women are too busy to truly appreciate the lives they've built. Many of these women feel profoundly disconnected as they mindlessly strive every day for more.

2. ***The "I Just Want (Fill in the Blank) and I'll be Happy" Woman.*** These women aim a little too low, setting their heights on only one goal. Once that's accomplished, they feel as if they're "done"—until something forces them to change. That perfect husband walks away from the marriage. Their ideal job is phased out. Or that perfect home is in foreclosure. These women often feel resentful and regretful, as if they haven't stretched their wings to the fullest capacity.

3. ***The "I Can Have Some of It, Some of the Time" Woman.*** This woman realizes that she can have it all, but over the course of a lifetime. For a period of time, she might focus on her career and leave other aspects of her life "on hold" for a bit. She doesn't totally dismiss those other areas, but her primary focus is singularly located for the time.

This woman reexamines her life periodically to see if she feels satisfied with the balance she's created for herself. Maybe she's feeling lonely and needs to work on her love life or expand her social network a bit more. Or she needs to feel more connected with her community and includes some charity work for her spiritual gratification.

This woman also understands that gratitude for what she *has* accomplished enriches her life; she's not always striving for more in the future, but spends time truly appreciating the now.

What type of woman are you? Probably, like most of us, a bit of each one. But that last type of woman lives with a deeper (and more realistic) sense of authenticity. She is staying true to herself, shaping and re-shaping herself as she sees fit, according to her inner picture. She makes decisions consciously and deliberately. She compares herself less with others and more with her previous self.

How Can I Discover What Is Authentic For Me?

There's no one formula for authenticity. It's going to be something different for everyone. For some, it might be about speaking up and finally finding your voice. For others, it can be the opposite: becoming a better listener instead of a big talker.

One thing is for sure: it's a journey that we all must go on, whether we like it or not. Some of us are still kicking and screaming or avoiding the situation all together. We know deep in our hearts that we must start that business, take that trip around the world, take that writing class, or go build that school in Africa, but we are so wrapped up in our fears that we allow our excuses to stop us from being our most authentic selves.

But until you listen to your heart and that deep inner voice, you are not going to find the freedom and happiness you not only desire but also deserve. As Shakti Gawain says, *"Every time you don't follow your inner guidance, you feel a loss of energy, loss of power, a sense of spiritual deadness."*

And so you need to set yourself free from the grip of fears and worries and start living the life you have always wanted. Yes, you will find many challenges along the way, but guess what? You will find challenges if you stay where you are as well. By taking the path of authenticity, you will have something the status quo will never give you—the rewards of knowing you followed your heart and your dreams. You will gain much more than you could ever lose.

Authenticity – My Personal Story

You must recognize and embrace all of who you are in order to experience your authentic self, your inner truth.

~ Iyanla Vanzant, *Tapping The Power Within*

Part of being authentic is following your intuition, your inner guidance system, even if (and this is the hard part!) you don't always understand where it's leading you. This is something I began to learn quite early in my life.

Back when I was in my teens, I felt so different from my family members that there were moments when I wondered if I was adopted. I was the proverbial black sheep of the family.

From a young age, I could tell that my thoughts and beliefs were different from my parents and my two siblings. Everything from the food I liked to my initial forays into spirituality raised my family's eyebrows. Secretly, I wondered whether I was more like my biological father. (My mother and biological father had separated when I was only a few months old, so I knew very little about him. My mother soon remarried and my stepfather raised me.)

Like many divorces, my parents did not end on good terms. My mother did her best to teach me the values and beliefs that she felt would prepare me for life. Unfortunately, I did not make it easy for her; I always made a point of disagreeing with her whenever possible.

When she became frustrated with my contrary attitude, she would threaten to send me to my biological father, who lived in another country, thousands of miles away. We laugh about it now but this threat left a strong impression on me. Instead of scaring me, it piqued my curiosity about my father. *What's my biological father like? Am I anything like him? Would he love and accept me for who I am? Would we get along?*

When I graduated from high school, I knew I had to spend time with him. The desire to get to know him made little sense to my family, but I just *knew* that's what I had to do. And I'm so glad I did. Living with my biological father allowed me to understand myself on a deeper level, one I hadn't imagined before.

It was frightening at first to move back to my home country of Brazil. I wasn't even sure if I would remember my first language, Portuguese. My father lived in Belo Horizonte, Brazil's third largest city, but it still felt too small for me. I felt like a foreigner in my own country.

But after some time with my father, I began to feel more comfortable. I realized he is both a brilliant and complicated man. And I saw myself in him in so many different ways—the good, the bad and the ugly. I couldn't believe how two people could live apart and still be so similar. As I understood him, I began to understand myself.

There were two traits where I saw myself clearly in my father. One excited and thrilled me while the other concerned me. The first was his insatiable hunger for knowledge. Some people nicknamed him "the walking encyclopedia." I remember times as a teenager, during our infrequent visits, when my sister and I would stay up all night hearing him talk about fascinating topics like psychology and spirituality.

It was during this time that my love and commitment for spiritual growth and empowerment was first awakened. He inspired a passion in me not only for learning but for sharing knowledge with others. This helped me find my path later in life and follow my calling.

The second trait I recognized in myself was his societal rebellion. My father had a huge distrust for society and all the values it forces upon us, the way it dictates who we should be, what we should do, where we should live, etc. (I remember a time when he didn't even want to have a checking account.)

Some of his views may have been a little radical, but I often had similar thoughts. My mother was a bit frightened to see them in me. She was concerned that I would also live, as she called it, "outside of society." To her, this was a lonely place to be and she feared for me.

Although I didn't admit it to my mother at the time, I felt concerned too. Why? Because I saw how my father's social aversions put a strain on his relationships and brought stress upon him. I knew then that I needed to find my *own* way to deal with my views of society, with a more positive twist.

I wanted to make people realize that it was okay to break away from the pack and still be part of the world as we know it. It's okay for us to disagree with our government, distrust certain corporate systems and live a different type of life than the commercially-saturated masses. In the same breath, we can embrace being part of communities and initiate change where we see fit, instead of shunning it all.

I'm grateful for the experiences I had while living with my dad. It helped me find my own answers and realize what I needed to do to fulfill my authentic life. Time with my biological father was one of the first instances where I felt power, true inner power. I was finally in the driver's seat of my life.

Steps to Genuine Authenticity

So are you ready to live a more authentic life? Here are the steps you can take to get started on the journey to greater authenticity right now:

- ***Be willing to be uncomfortable for a while.*** Interestingly, the overarching step to getting closer to your true authentic self is less about doing and more about being. Doing less to get to your core self might feel foreign at first; we are so used to wearing those masks that we're unsure who we are without them. But like any practice, we get used to our innate stillness. We welcome it.

- ***Learn to enjoy your own company again.*** Most people are not able to be alone in a room by themselves. They need to have either the TV or their phone. How are you able to listen to your inner voice if there's noise surrounding you all the time? Take some time each day to spend alone. But be conscious of this time, not busy. Allow yourself to feel the discomfort and the pleasure it may evoke.

- ***Learn to be a witness to your own life.*** Start becoming an observer of your own life, instead of a constantly active player. If there's a challenging situation in your life, see if you can look at it from a distance, without all the emotional force behind it. Can you take a mental break from your worries and just breathe and be at peace?

You can ask yourself the following questions:

- *How are other's opinions shaping my actions?*
- *Am I taking things too personally?*
- *Am I in contact with energy vampires that drain and exhaust me?*
- *Am I in touch with my feelings?*
- *Do I need to cry or share my feelings with someone?*
- *Am I in my body or do I feel disconnected?*

Ask these questions as a scientist would, without all of the emotional volatility.

- ***Become aware of your thoughts.*** Sometimes our thoughts are our greatest enemies. We give too much credence to them, treating them like bold-faced facts. A thought is just a thought. By questioning them, especially your negative ones, you grow closer to the source: the real you. Often, we're berating ourselves casually. Catch those thoughts and toss them in the trash.

- ***Revisit your core desires.*** Reflect back on your life.

  - *What are your natural likes and dislikes?*
  - *What are you passionate about?*
  - *What morals have always meant a lot to you?*
  - *What makes you feel comfortable?*
  - *When do you "lose yourself"?*

(Cultivating awareness is key in this process. Consider it a personal life inventory. Reflect and seek out. Write it down. Paint that canvas.)

- ***Practice saying "no" more often.*** For women, this is particularly difficult but entirely necessary. Those boundaries you create become the foundation for true authenticity.

- ***Take care of yourself first.*** And limit your caretaking. Women can often become hooked on caretaking, thinking (subconsciously at least) that it proves they are needed. Resentment can easily creep in if you're working too hard to save the world.

- ***List 3 things you love doing but haven't done in a long time.*** Get your schedule out and make some time for each activity. Notice how you feel when you do the things you love, as well as when you follow through with a promise made to yourself.

- ***Buy a large piece of butcher paper at your local store.*** Gather different magazines and start cutting images of things that call out to you and that you would like to manifest in your life. Glue them on to your paper and start visualizing them coming into your life. This is your vision board. Make sure you look at it every day.

- ***Stop the lies.*** You're probably saying, "What, me? I don't lie." But women do…and frequently. We say we're feeling fine when we're not. We couch our opinions to protect the feelings of others. We downplay our anger when deep inside, we want to scream. Experiment with a 24-hour "truthfest." Speak up, speak out, speak your mind. Catch yourself in those "white lies" we've become too accustomed to uttering.

- ***Accept your truth and allow others to live their truth as well.*** We are all entitled to our own truth. Judging others can also sway you from your authentic self. It's important to view the world *as is*, without creating judgments based on the way you think it should be.

- ***Practice total and complete presence in the moment.*** You can't be authentic and in touch with your inner essence, when you are not present in the here and now. Meditation is a great practice to guide you back to the present moment.

Inner Reflections

- Who are you? How would you describe yourself to a complete stranger? Avoid defining yourselves by your roles. Focus on the qualities of your being.

- What inspires you? What songs? Books? Movies? What women? Why?

- What makes you feel the most alive in this world?

- If you only had one week to live, what would you do right now? How would it change your life priorities?

- Describe a time when you felt completely authentic and true to yourself, with no fears about what others might say. If you've never had such a time, write a fantasy in which you imagine what that time might be like.

My Insights

Write down any thoughts and feelings that might have come up for you while reading this chapter.

Go to www.PowerVirtues.com/Authenticity to continue your journey of *Embracing Authenticity.*

CHAPTER 3
Uncovering Sensuality

To be sensual, I think, is to respect and rejoice in the force of life, of life itself, and to be present in all that one does, from the effort of loving to the making of bread.

~ James Arthur

What is Sensuality?

What images arise when you think of a sensual woman? Do you think of a thin, blond, attractive-looking young woman? Or perhaps you might envision an empowered, radiant female who simply feels good about herself, no matter what size or shape?

What else is sensual to you? A luscious strawberry or a hot, sandy beach? A whisper or a gentle touch? A hot bath or a hot fudge sundae? A secret, knowing glance or a morning bird singing?

As you read this chapter, I'd like to ask you to keep an open mind and suspend erroneous concepts you may have picked up about sensuality along the way. (Not to worry—most of us have!)

There are several definitions for the word sensuality. Most are connected to sexuality, but that narrow definition reflects the limited perspective so prevalent in our society. For many centuries, we have been told that our sensual or sexual expression is either dirty or dangerous. Sexuality and sensuality became interconnected and considered wrong somehow.

In today's world, it's as if our sensual self only exists when we're having sex. And therein lies the problem: we deny ourselves the range of daily opportunities to feel sensual on our own, without a partner.

Sexuality & Sensuality - The Difference

Loosely defined, sexuality is a person's sexual orientation or preference. It relates to specific sexual interaction with a partner. Sensuality is a subtle and internal state of mind that you experience deep inside yourself. And it's accessible at any time, with or without another person.

Sensuality derives from the word "sense," which means to feel. What it really means is "feeling" with all of your senses: sight, sound, smell, taste and touch (as well as your intuition or sixth sense). When you are living sensually, you are fully engaged with your senses. This means a deeper, richer sense of presence and joy in your life.

Many women don't take the time or energy to focus on sensuality. Our busy days don't often allow for it, it seems. But when you begin to take the time to experience your sensual side, you'll end up accomplishing more in less time —and enjoy what you're doing more as well.

Why? Because a sensual woman is aware; she's awake to all that is going on around her. She's not locked in a frenetic mindset or grieving over her past. She's here, now. She's drinking in the world around her and can act from a more prepared state. Think of a cat. This sensual creature can be relaxed and enjoying the sun yet pounce at a moment's notice.

The same holds true with us: sensuality opens us up to life and helps us live more in the present. We're ready to "pounce" when needed, too!

The Pleasure Principle

As I mentioned, many of us equate sensuality with sexual pleasure. But there are many ways in which to experience sensual pleasure other than in the bedroom. We require a degree of pleasure in almost all aspects of our life, whether we're aware of it or not. If we don't experience it, we begin to feel empty inside and our energy becomes depleted.

When we feel little pleasure at work, we have a hard time getting through the day. When there's no pleasure in our food, we feel denied and often overeat (or undereat) in response. When we feel no sensual gratification looking at our image in the mirror, we have a hard time feeling relaxed in our own skin.

The goal of this chapter is to look at the entirety of your life, from the moment you wake in the morning until you go to sleep at night (even in your dreams), from a sensual perspective. At this very moment, what could you do to increase your sensual experience? Sip a hot cup of fragrant tea? Brush your hair with awareness? Put on a cozy sweater? Listen to a gentle piece of music?

This isn't about simply feeling good; sensuality can be a tool for our empowerment, launching us forward into the lives we want to live.

Why Is There Power In Sensuality?

Women today are extremely over-committed, juggling a hundred things at once. We get so caught up in the hustle and bustle that we're left with little to no time to take care of ourselves and meet our deeper needs.

And we so easily forgo those needs. We don't honor or recognize the direct correlation between our sensual side and the rest of our lives. Yet sensuality offers an immediate way to connect with our deepest desires. When we invite sensuality into our lives, our intuition becomes heightened. Our joy exponentially increases. Our sense of self is awakened. Sensuality is a short cut to your authentic self.

Sensuality is also inextricably entwined with our femininity. And sometimes, reconnecting with our sense of femininity can take a little soul searching. Our world is so dominated by masculine energy that the "yin" side of ourselves seems to be hiding in a closet somewhere, covering her ears from all the commotion.

Start by defining your personal "brand" of sensuality. What has it meant to you in the past? Now? When do you feel the most feminine? Aware of all of your senses? Are you walking alone on the beach or eating a sumptuous meal? Are you eating fresh raspberries or whispering in your lover's ear?

By doing this inventory, you rekindle your memory and your subconscious begins to look for similar situations in your everyday experience. Perhaps you can't walk on the beach, but the air blowing through your hair while driving home feels magical. Or sipping on lemony iced tea in the backyard is heavenly.

As you read this book, what kind of sensual pleasures are you experiencing? Maybe it's a comfortable pair of jeans you're wearing or the feel of sun pouring through the window? Perhaps some beautiful music is playing through your speakers? (Music is always a quick and easy way to access your sensuality.) Take a moment to bathe in your current sensual triggers.

As you reconnect with your own personal brand of femininity, you will understand that you have different needs than men, as well as other women. You alone know when and how you need to recharge yourself sensually to feel your best. This means recognizing when you feel stressed or disconnected and shifting your focus to your sensual needs. What would it take to make you feel more replenished? A hug? A bath? Sex? Sleep? (Yes, sleeping can be a very sensual act.)

Recharging your sensual side builds your feminine power. Your soul feels fortified. You become a strong, sensual woman, ready to take on the world and thoroughly drink in every moment of your life.

Sensuality and Safety

We have routinely been taught to fear our pleasure over the years. Masturbation is dirty, too much sex is slutty, too little is prudish. It's high time to trade in those outmoded, destructive ways of thinking. Our sensuality is one of the most empowering tools we possess. We have access to faculties we never knew existed and we become unstoppable, living in our fullness.

Though there's an important caveat: it's very difficult for women to surrender to their sensuality if they don't feel safe. If they feel they might become the target of abuse and exploitation (which history has shown us repeatedly), they will repress their sensuality and lose their power yet again.

For a long time, I possessed a lot of fear when it came to feeling safe and protected. Throughout my life, I've had bad feelings—even visions—of being attacked by a man from behind or someone breaking into my house. I usually brushed it off, thinking it was residual paranoia brought on by my childhood sexual abuse. But then I went to an event that opened my eyes to the reality of living life as a woman.

There were about 3,000 people in the room and half of them were women. The speaker asked the women who had felt concerned about their safety in the last week to stand up. I was one of the first to stand and simply stunned to see that almost all of the women joined me. You could hear a pin drop.

He then asked the men the same question. Only five men rose. That was a huge awakening moment for me. I realized how much we fear for our safety routinely.

So how do you feel safe again so you can explore your sensuality? This is a very important question and one that only you can answer. You must search yourself and your history. Uncover those fears and look at the source. And unfortunately, this is no easy task. Many of us have experienced abuse in various forms: verbal, physical or sexual abuse, for instance. We proceed on, as we must, but the fear remains, like a monster hiding under the bed.

Deep personal work is often required to free yourself from those rusty chains. This may mean therapy, journaling, meditation, prayer, research, spiritual retreats; there is no one method to heal old pain and fear. One thing *is* for sure: if you do nothing about it, it will remain. That kind of pain needs to be addressed or it simply replays itself in various destructive forms.

Sensuality is essentially about freedom; the freedom of being who you are; the freedom to create yourself from deep within; the freedom to release yourself from old pain and live fully once again.

Awaken Your Senses Again

Many of us take our senses for granted. They just "do their job" with little to no notice. Wake up and connect with the inner workings of your senses again, as you did when you were a child. Take a moment to fully embrace the world around you. Note what your eyes naturally gravitate toward, which smells stimulate you, what feels good against your skin.

How do you feel in your own body? In order to reconnect to your senses, you must feel good in your body: relaxed, ready, open. Are you feeling connected or does stress hold you back from a truly sensual life? What keeps you from experiencing your sensual side? Stress and fatigue are often the causes.

But like any other bad habit, a little retraining is needed. Take the time to bathe in the sensual experiences that surround you every day. It starts in the morning by noticing how good your coffee tastes and ends by curling up on soft flannel sheets for a sound night's sleep. Notice how you feel rejuvenated, connected and alive simply by taking in the pleasures that abound. As you reconnect with your senses, your spiritual awareness will increase naturally.

You'll see a new you emerge: vibrant, passionate, engaged in the world. It's fascinating that our senses hold so much power, but they do. And they are always there, waiting for you.

The Sensuality Soul Dance

The fastest way for most women to connect with their bodies and their sensuality is through dance. No surprise, right? We all know how good dance can feel. Nothing can awaken your femininity more than moving your body, especially your hips, which is where your feminine energy originates.

Dancing is a way to transport yourself into a whole different dimension, free of your thoughts, beliefs and preconceived notions. I'm not referring to the type of dance we witness at a nightclub or at a ballroom dance class, although these might be good ways to get started.

The dance I'm referring to is what I like to call "soul dancing" or "trance dancing", as it's occasionally been called. It's deeper, more intimate. The best part? No lessons required! Just about every woman has danced in her own bedroom at some point. You turned up the music and sang loudly and danced just the way you wanted. No one was watching so there was no self-consciousness. You just released. This kind of dancing takes you on an inner journey to your soul, where you can access all the answers you are looking for in your life.

I have no recollection of when I started soul dancing; I just remember that it came naturally to me. Years later, I read about it and studied it with experts who practiced similar types of dance.

Nothing has felt so powerful for me. I'm not exaggerating when I tell you that soul dancing can change your life. Many times, I would stop dancing because my body would vibrate at such a powerful level that I became scared and didn't know what to do; I didn't understand what was happening inside of me.

The problem is that most women never allow themselves to experience this feeling. Why do we deny ourselves such a powerful, transformative force when it's so accessible?

My answer, after years of reflecting on it: we fear the power it creates in us. It is our sensual side, unleashed in movement. Full, unbridled expression. The powerful sensations racing through our body are often foreign to us. We feel threatened and disconnect from them.

Also, soul dancing is such a strong, feminine type of power and unfortunately, foreign in our society. We are much more used to the masculine model of power. It takes courage to experience this amount of feminine power. We might need to start slowly, but we need to start experiencing it nonetheless.

If this concept feels utterly foreign to you, consider taking some dance classes at your local dance studio. I highly recommend belly dancing. It's one of the most feminine and sensual dances on the planet and it will get you in touch with your sensuality in a heartbeat.

Dance is highly personal, so if you don't feel that "fit" after a few classes, move on! Most of us know the kind of dance we secretly long to learn. Ballet? Modern dance? Tango? Samba?

If a class feels daunting, then try a DVD in the privacy of your own home. Or turn up your stereo and get moving! Just allow yourself some time to find that place inside that compels you to move. Let your body do the talking. Gently move your head or your hands and arms in a way that feels most natural to you and the music.

Or wait and let the dance arise out of you. The most important part is that your movement is coming from an inner urge to express. It's completely unscripted, unrehearsed and 100% authentic. It should feel as if your body is moving you, not you moving your body. The movement emanates from a higher intelligence that knows exactly how it wants to move. You'll learn to trust it and access it more easily each time.

Ready to take it up a notch? Next time you are home by yourself, turn off the lights. Play your favorite type of sensual music and dance naked around your house or room. (If you do this during the full moon, it doubles the power!)

Just remember: this is not about getting it right. For some, it will take some time to find this side of ourselves once again. Just allow for "mistakes" or even that sense of not feeling it. The more you try, the easier it will be to access that soul dancer inside of you.

Steps to Living in Sensuality

Soul dancing is just one way to get in touch with your sensual side. A sensual experience is usually within arm's reach. Here are some other simple, accessible techniques to aid you.

- ***Take a sensory walk.*** Nothing wakes up the sensual side like being outdoors. Focus on the effect fresh air has on your awareness or the feeling of sunshine on your face. Breathe in deeply. Be fully present in your body and comfortable in your skin. Walks are highly transformative and easy to integrate into your life. (Nobody feels worse after a walk!)

- ***Turn all your senses on by taking a long, hot bath.*** Apply a couple of drops of your favorite scented oils to the water. Light up some candles or incense. Play your favorite relaxing and sensual music. If it feels right, invite your partner to join you. (Just remember, it's not necessarily about having a sexual encounter but experiencing your senses deeply with another.)

- ***Go for a weekend or weeklong retreat/spa and pamper yourself and your senses.*** This is dedicated time, especially tailored for your sensual side. We all need that kind of longer-term sensual submersion. If this seems cost-prohibitive, create a weekend at home loaded with sensual pleasures, dedicated to the enhancement of your sensory side.

- ***Look at yourself in the mirror and tell yourself "I love you!"*** Every single woman is beautiful and sexy in her own way. Notice the aspects you like about yourself and tell that "other" voice to be quiet. Drink in your sexiest qualities. Celebrate them.

- ***Give yourself the gift of a photo shoot so you can have proof of how beautiful you are.*** We often scrutinize our looks to the smallest detail and focus only on our worst aspects. A professional photographer is a third party who can easily show you how beautiful you really are.

- ***Eat with consciousness.*** Most of us rush our meals. We're disconnected when we eat. And you can guess the problems it causes: we overeat, undereat or have dietary problems. Slow it down and deliberately savor every single bite, taking the time to allow all of your senses to experience the food.

Inner Reflections

- How sensual do you feel on a daily basis? How connected are you to your sensuality? What disconnects you?

- What did you learn about sensuality growing up?

- What is your strongest sense: smell, touch, see, feel, hear? Your weakest? Which one would you like to strengthen?

- How comfortable do you feel in your body?

- What would it take for you to connect with your sensuality?

- What type of music makes you feel good? What other sounds arouse your sensual side?

My Insights

Write down any thoughts and feelings that might have come up for you while reading this chapter.

Go to www.PowerVirtues.com/Sensuality to continue your journey of *Uncovering Sensuality.*

CHAPTER 4
Discovering Spirituality

The great work that is beginning is the realization of the feminine as the bridge between God and humankind.

~ Marion Woodman, *Bone: Dying into Life*

What is Spirituality?

Ah, the million-dollar question. Defining spirituality is like describing love. Or grace. It can be a beautifully elusive process.

For some, spirituality can be found while strolling through the woods on a crisp autumn day or taking in a sunset at the beach. For others, giving to people in need or gathering with others to meditate or pray can be profoundly spiritual. It's a highly personal and transcendent process—one constantly evolving, like an ever-budding flower.

Many people equate spirituality with religion. But that's not quite right. While spirituality can be a component of religion, religion isn't necessarily part of spirituality.

Years ago, I had a feeling that these two concepts were essentially different, but I struggled with how to express it. Then I discovered a quote from author Iyanla Vanzant, where she put into words exactly what I always felt.

In *Tapping the Power Within*, she writes:

Religion offers a way, the rules and regulations, to approach the concept of God.

She goes on to explain:

Spirituality, on the other hand, means that you recognize, accept and are aligned in your individual connection to the Creator and use that spiritual connection as your guiding force.

The God Search

For a long time, I harbored a lot of resentment toward religion and the whole "God" concept. Growing up in a Catholic household, I thought God was a powerful, old man with a long white beard and a robe, sitting on the clouds, judging everything I did and ready to punish me at every step. No wonder I was angry with him!

Fortunately, I didn't remain stuck in anger for long. I searched for my own connection with my Creator or God. (Whatever you call your spiritual guidance doesn't really matter.) I certainly had no idea what to call it at first or even what this relationship might look like. I just knew there must be something out there bigger than myself.

So what did I discover on my quest? I learned that spirituality is an inner journey, while religion (for the most part) is an external process. You are obeying God's law as taught to you from a third party. Spirituality is about going within and listening to an inner god. It's a calling to the center of your soul. No middleman involved!

Spirituality also reminds us that we are not alone on this journey called Life. It sounds so simple but it's incredibly profound and comforting: we are all in this together, connected by life's experiences.

My first glimpse of this oneness with others came when I attended my first personal development workshop and realized that what I was going through was not unique; many were going through similar dilemmas. Once I understood that I wasn't alone, I was finally able to step out of the confusion I had harbored for so long.

When Religion and Spirituality Collide - My Story

Religion separates us, spirituality brings us together.

~ Dr. Wayne Dyer

For as long as I can remember, spirituality has been very important to me, even though I wasn't sure where my spiritual beliefs originated. Maybe they came from my grandmother, whom I saw praying several times a day, carrying saint figurines everywhere she went. Or perhaps it was my parents, who were open-minded and encouraged me to experience spirituality and religion in my own way.

But ultimately, I think my spirituality stemmed from a much deeper place—a place we can all go where we silence our minds and hear the voice of our inner truth. This place has no right or wrong, just peace, where you are free to explore your true feelings and thoughts without judgment or outside influences.

At a young age, I discovered this place and spent as much time as I could there. I read voraciously about spiritual matters. I prayed and meditated. I looked to the stars for hours on end. I can't say I found all the answers I was looking for. In fact, sometimes I found more questions than answers. But that was fine; it was more important to explore and discover what spirituality really meant for me.

As I grew up, I developed a passion for studying different religions and cultures. I wanted to understand what other people did to find their "god." But my real spiritual journey began when I met my husband-to-be.

He was everything I ever dreamt of in a man: strong, smart, charming, caring, sensitive, loving and incredibly handsome. It was like I had made a secret wish list of all the qualities I wanted in a man and the Universe had delivered me my order!

There was one factor that I had not planned for; he was from a very different religious background than mine. Me: a Brazilian immigrant with a Catholic background, studying in American schools. He: a Lebanese immigrant living in England, raised a Muslim. We couldn't be more different...or so I thought.

At first, I was concerned that our religious differences would inevitably separate us. *How would we relate to each other on a daily basis? Would our families get along? What would our wedding ceremony look like? How would we raise our children?*

These questions raced through my mind as I looked into the eyes of the man of my dreams.

Although I had moments of fear and confusion, something inside of me was stronger: the love I was beginning to feel for this man. Every part of my soul knew that we were meant to be together, so how could I let something like religion get in the way?

Reconciling our different backgrounds turned out to be much easier than I thought. Perhaps it was the power of our love or the determination of our spirits, but we soon realized that, despite our religious differences, we were more alike than different. We both believed in something higher than ourselves, and what we called it didn't really matter. More importantly, we focused on our love and the love we wanted to share with the world. That's when I began to understand what true spirituality is really about and started to live it on a daily basis.

In the end, my husband and I discovered that it's more important that our religion adapts to us, not the other way around. So many people create their own interpretation of religion and use it for their own self-serving purposes. Some use it to create wars while others use it to exert power over others. Why not use it to benefit humanity and create a shared religion based on love and respect for one another? Our world would be much more peaceful.

The moral of my story? Don't be afraid to create your own "religion." Let it set you free from the chains of self-doubt and self-loathing. Make it into something that empowers and inspires you to become a better person every day—not just for yourself but for the world. That's when you can begin to live spirituality, not just study or talk about it.

Why is Spirituality Particularly Important for Women?

As I mentioned earlier, I have always been a spiritual seeker. I read piles and piles of books and spent thousands of dollars on workshops and one-on-one guidance. And because of my focus on growth and self-improvement, my life eventually expanded to a level I never thought possible. I was truly grateful for the level of awareness I had achieved and the breakthroughs I experienced. Still, something was missing.

Then it hit me like a lightning bolt: I realized that religion didn't really understand women...and I am one! This was another contributing factor to my disconnection from it.

How could religion include women when the ones creating all of the rules were men? Where was the female perspective? It seemed religion cared more about dominating women than the evolution of our souls. Did *any* religion stem from a woman's perspective? What could they be teaching me?

I began to search for female spiritual teachers and I did find a few, but not many. This is an area where we women must step up. We must define who we are as spiritual beings. No one is going to do that for us. This is our responsibility. It's our time to reclaim who we are spiritually and gain our power back.

I was reminded of this when I read Theresa King's book, *The Spiral Path*, a beautiful piece about women's spirituality. I was particularly touched when King said:

> *Our spirituality must be truly holistic. It must speak to all those parts of us that make us woman as well as the parts that make us human...Women need to find such spirituality. This task requires courage, of course, and brutal honesty. We need to deeply question what we*

> *have been taught to believe, to reinterpret truths on which we have been raised, and to examine our ideas to see if they really 'fit' – if they are indeed leading us to self-enlightenment and full maturity.*

This is not an easy task, but if we don't take on this responsibility, the consequences are a lack of deep and rich fulfillment in our lives. And potentially worse, the generations of women to come will continue to feel that emptiness in their hearts without knowing why.

It's all right to search your religion of origin (if you have one) and see what you can take with you on your path. I believe all religions have something beautiful to offer at their core. Religions teach us that there are things we should do, laws we must obey. Life can be pretty chaotic with no rules.

But we must be wary and discriminating: religion can often be loaded with too many rules that ultimately limit us and bleed into other aspects of our lives. We become paralyzed by indecision ("*Am I doing the right thing*?") or do things we'd prefer not to do ("*I should go to that work party or they'll think I don't care about my job*"). If we feel that we have made the wrong decision, self-punishment ensues, often much more severe than needed.

This vicious cycle of "shouldness" slowly squelches that deeper spiritual voice, the one waiting to gently guide us. It is only from following that quiet feminine voice that we develop our real power. (But it's often hard to hear that voice when so many other inner voices are yelling at us!)

Once we reconnect to our inner spirit, decisions seem to answer themselves. Self-admonishment is replaced with a sense of confidence in our decision-making. We're more at peace with ourselves. Faith and trust replace doubt and anxiety.

How to Become a Spiritual Feminine Warrior Again

Women are natural healers, teachers, warriors and nurturers, yet many of us have forgotten this truth. As we return to spirituality, we begin to experience these qualities again. As we return to spirituality, we begin to heal ourselves and other women. A cosmic ripple effect occurs.

The first step to empowering yourself with spirituality is to cultivate that deep inner knowing that tells you there's something bigger than yourself, something guiding you. This something is a part of you, flowing inside of you.

I had once heard, "To think there is no greater power than ourselves is akin to believing a bestselling book magically appears after an explosion in the printing shop." How can the spectacular nature of life, the mystery and wonder of it all, not have something going on behind the scenes?

There is a greater power at work, all the time. When we close our eyes and see the world through our inner vision, we are able to connect with this amazing power, sometimes without even realizing it. It's present in the mother who knows when her child is in danger, in the corporate executive that says no to a deal that seemed perfect but actually could have bankrupted the company, in every woman who yearns for something more in her life, and by visualizing it, obtains it. This power is at our disposal *now*.

There are many tools we can use to connect with it; religion is simply one of them. What's important to remember is that the path you create for yourself—forged in love, healing, understanding, service, and growth—must resonate with you.

It's an amazing sense of freedom you experience when you begin to realize that there is something greater than just your mere physical being. You are part of something so much bigger than yourself. You are co-creating your life.

Oprah Winfrey once said something that deeply moved me:

> *"How I think one masters one's life is to understand that you are co-creating that life with the Ultimate Creator. Not understanding that puts you at your own pitiful, meager, little will and everything is left up to you. And you can't do it. You cannot survive in this world by yourself, just believing in yourself. You're not big enough to do it. I'm not big enough to do it. Nobody is big enough to do it."*

I've often struggled with the idea that I'm completely on my own, that it's up to me to make my life happen (a masculine frame of mind). That I need to *do* in order to *be*. That I must climb a ladder in order to succeed. And I'm all alone in the process.

This belief drained me. But when I remember the truth of my feminine spiritual nature and connect with the source of all life, my day just flows and my energy is revitalized. The doors open up and life is no longer a struggle. The challenges still rear their heads, trust me. But now, I have a resource to draw upon.

It's also validating to think that someone as successful and actualized as Oprah Winfrey believes in a higher power who guides and helps her. It reminds me that I can find continued success and guidance through my higher power; it's beyond a standard masculine-centric approach to think that the only way to "win" is through struggle and on my own.

In the book *Tapping the Power Within*, author Iyanla Vanzant discusses a simple way to look at life and spirituality. She teaches us that there are three ways to look at the circumstances in our lives: we are basically either teaching a lesson, learning a lesson or we are the object of a lesson. Most of the time when we are teaching a lesson, we are also learning a lesson as well.

For example, you could be the child of parents who weren't very emotionally expressive. Their stiffness and stoicism often made you feel underloved. You can still use this opportunity to learn. When you get older, for example, you might work diligently to develop an emotionally open and flexible self, in spite of your earlier modeling.

In essence, we are here to grow and evolve as human beings and so-called negative situations are here to help us do just that.

Letting Go of Our Stories and Our Stuff

One of the biggest obstacles on our spiritual path is our attachment to the physical world. We cling desperately to our identities, thoughts and beliefs. We create stories in our heads about life that are often askew. We live with filters that don't allow us to see things for what they really are. Filters blind us from the truth, our inner truth.

Most of us have had this experience: you interpreted a situation to mean one thing, only to find out later you were totally off-course. We fret and worry and play these types of internal recordings in our head over and over again, many times a day. What stories are stuck in your head? Do you know what it would feel like to be free of them?

We are also very attached to our material things. And while there is nothing wrong with wanting to have money and the possessions it can buy, we can often feel that we are nothing without them. Money and material things are here to serve us, not the other way around. Don't become a slave to things that matter so little in your life. Enjoy them and release your attachment to them.

How to Harness the Power of Spirit

Now that you know the difference between religion and spirituality and understand how growing your spiritual side can drastically improve your life, are you ready to take the dive?

Here are a few suggestions to get your spirit wheel turning:

- ***Join a group or community that inspires you.*** You can easily find hundreds of local groups on the internet, from traditional prayer meetings to meditation "meet-ups." The important thing is to find something that is meaningful to you.

- ***Surround yourself with women that inspire and uplift you.*** Most of us are in toxic environments, especially if you work a 9 - 5 job where people are often unhappy. Sooner or later, we start feeling completely drained and exhausted. By connecting with people who inspire and empower us, we collectively detox our negative thoughts and feelings, staying true to what's real in our lives. Feel free to join our own free online community of supportive and visionary women at www.FeminineSoul.com.

- ***Practice meditation and prayer every day.*** Don't be intimidated by the word "meditation" or even the word "prayer." For each of us this can mean something different. Feel free to define it in whatever way feels comfortable to you. What's important is that you spend a few minutes in silence and solitude every day to connect with a deeper part of you, and from that place, ask for what you want.

- ***Start a journal and spend 10 - 15 minutes a day quietly writing.*** Don't edit your writing; just keep writing for 15 minutes. Let your thoughts just pour onto the paper. You will be amazed at how much insight you will begin to have through this regular practice.

- ***Find a cause that you believe in and start supporting it.*** If your schedule doesn't allow you to donate your time, you can make financial contributions. (But participation is always preferred!)

- ***Allow yourself to be guided by your intuition, by spirit.*** Align your thinking mind with your spiritual essence and listen to your inner guidance system. Note when you have a "gut instinct" about something and be thankful for it. The more you recognize that side of yourself, the more it grows.

- ***Let go of your ego and reach for faith in something bigger than yourself.*** Be gentle with yourself; this doesn't happen overnight. Remember that the ego doesn't want you to be happy. But the ego is only an illusion that we can strive to break free from, if we work at it every day. Learn to let go and release into your higher power.

- ***Believe in yourself and know that you are not alone.*** That higher power is always there with you. All you have to do is close your eyes and feel it. Connect with it on a daily basis. It's an inner journey where only your heart is allowed to roam. So let go of your thinking mind and your ego for a bit! They're not invited.

- ***Start noticing and appreciating the beauty in all of life***, including yourself, no matter where you have been and what you have done in the past, no matter how you feel. My mother used to always say: "Only museums live in the past." Let go of your past and drink in the here and now.

- ***Develop a practice of connecting with your Creator, whomever or whatever that may be for you***, as long as it's something that empowers you. Be diligent, conscious and consistent about it. Like a muscle, it strengthens with use and atrophies when ignored.

Inner Reflections

- What does spirituality mean to you?

- How do you experience spirituality?

- Which spiritual path calls out to you?

- What do you think is your life's "calling?" (What do you feel called to do as opposed to what you feel you *should* do?)

- What do you want from spirituality? What are your spiritual goals?

My Insights

Write down any thoughts and feelings that might have come up for you while reading this chapter.

Go to www.PowerVirtues.com/Spirituality to continue your journey of *Discovering Spirituality.*

CHAPTER 5
Cultivating Gratitude

Gratitude is not only the greatest of virtues but the parent of all others.

~ Cicero

What is Real Gratitude?

If you've read any New Age books, you've undoubtedly stumbled across the term "gratitude." We've heard about its importance repeatedly. We've been instructed to write lists filled with thankfulness. But do we really understand the need for gratitude? Do we know how to practice it simply and practically in our everyday life so it makes a *real* difference?

Gratitude is the spiritual glue that ties all of the other Power Virtues together. When you discover core gratitude, the other virtues become easily accessible to you.

Living from a place of gratitude means being present in the moment and not taking anything or anyone for granted. It means experiencing life as a gift and cherishing it wholeheartedly. Are you focusing on what you appreciate about your life or simply what's wrong with it?

When you are able to tap into genuine appreciation, you have the ability to transform any situation in your life, whether it's an argument with a loved one or a difficult work situation.

It might be a conscious effort at first, like a baby's first steps. We're all trained to focus on what's wrong with a situation. But with practice, you'll feel the benefits of being in a more positive and grateful place.

So What *are* The Benefits Of Gratitude?

- Gratitude bolsters your self-esteem. When you feel thankful, you tend to feel better about yourself.
- Gratitude connects you with your spiritual essence and reminds us that we're all connected.
- Your true essence is found through gratitude. You become more authentic and open.
- A state of gratitude brings you into the present. You learn to accept *what is* now.
- You recognize that your life is full of blessings, so nagging negativity and dangerous stress fall easily by the wayside.
- The people in your life feel more appreciated and tend to appreciate you more.

- On a cosmic scale, gratitude sends out a psychic ripple effect. You contribute to a more positive Universe.

Gratitude - My Story

Living in gratitude definitely didn't happen for me overnight. During my younger years, I was brimming with anger. I was angry with myself for not excelling at school or being impatient with my mom or unsure of myself for being overweight or for not having a boyfriend, or disliking the one I had. Gratitude certainly wasn't in my vocabulary.

I spent those early years slipping in and out of depression. It had become a way of life for me. And the sad part? I was getting used to it. I had become an expert whiner and complainer. I made my mom's life a living hell during this time. All of my troubles were her fault and she often experienced the brunt of my abrasiveness. Deep inside, I knew that even if my troubles were to suddenly disappear, I wouldn't notice. They were living, breathing entities permanently camped out in my head. In short, I *was* my problem.

When I graduated from high school, I left home. (Finally, I could escape the source of all evil!) Little did I know that the next four years would be a crash course in Appreciation at the University of Life. I went back to my country of origin, Brazil, where suddenly I had to support myself and take on adult responsibility. Whining turned into working.

I began to appreciate my parents in a way I never had before. Although I had relatives around me, it wasn't the same as home. I reflected back longingly at every holiday I had ever spent with my family. The holidays were always happy times. My mother made the most delicious Brazilian meals and the house felt especially warm and cozy. We'd dress up to the hilt and dance the night away to Samba music. Any problems would be forgotten and we were as one. Through this time of reflection, I realized I needed to do a little less complaining and a lot more living and loving.

For a while, this new sense of appreciation permeated every area of my life. I would wake up with a prayer in my heart and fall asleep with thoughts of gratitude. It was a time that I felt deeply connected with everyone and everything around me. The troubles I encountered were just stepping stones to get me where I needed to go.

I would love to tell you that it stayed like that for the next 20 years, but it didn't. All of us go through circumstances that bring us to our knees. For me, it was the divorce from my first husband. Everything I had learned about gratitude went right out the window, and I dove deep into depression. It was one of the hardest times of my life, but every fiber of my being knew that this divorce was needed. The one thing that helped me move through those dark times was the knowledge that my pain was a means to an end; it would ultimately make me stronger.

Most of us know it's easy to feel grateful when everything is running smoothly. It's during those heartbreaking, soul-trying moments that you must flex your gratitude muscles by searching deep inside for something–*anything*–to appreciate. During my divorce, my gratitude list was pretty short. But I continued to focus on the small things, like walks on the beach and feeling the cool salt air on my face. So yes, my life challenges were there—trust me, they were looming–I just made room for some gratitude amidst it all. If we can begin to accept the circumstances at hand and remember that everything has a higher purpose, we set the foundation for a life based on gratitude.

There is always a blessing behind every challenge. And sometimes the blessing can't be seen right away. Months, sometimes years, can go by before we see "the gift within the wound." But it is always there. Without my divorce, for instance, I would have never met my second husband (who is truly my soul mate) only three short years later.

But obviously, life isn't a happily ever after story. My new relationship wasn't peaches and cream at first. We lived over 3,000 miles away from each other for the first seven months of our relationship. He was going through a traumatic divorce himself. We certainly acquired our share of scratches and bruises along the way but that only made us stronger and more grateful to have one another.

My second husband once said that he wished we had met ten years earlier. I told him if that had happened, I probably would not appreciate him the way I do now. The reason we have such a strong, solid and passionate relationship is because of the experiences we had before we met each other. So gratitude is a process; it's not a destination. There's a big picture you must always keep in mind. A certain amount of faith in the future outcome must remain in your heart.

The Power of Giving Thanks

In 2002, I took over the management of a boutique hotel in the heart of London. The work environment was hostile, something I was not used to. Regardless, I made sure I showed my deepest appreciation to everyone working there, whether it was a high-level executive, the receptionist or the janitor.

This was particularly challenging because renovations were being done in the building by a group of workers who spoke very little English. But just like love and kindness, gratitude is a universal language. They got the message. After a while, they would point to their work, smile, then ask me in their broken English, "Good job?" "Of course," I would reply, "Great job!"

After a couple of weeks, everyone noticed a huge difference in employee morale. It had become a much better place to work every day. We all need to feel valued and appreciated in some way.

It takes so little to give this priceless gift to others yet most of us don't do it often enough. Sometimes we feel embarrassed to express ourselves. During those moments of self-consciousness, remind yourself that an act of gratitude is not about you but about the other person. Gratitude has a ripple effect. Throw your stone in the pond unabashedly.

I once attended a workshop where gratitude and appreciation were the core topics. One of the exercises was to make a list of all the people in our lives for whom we needed to show our appreciation, including those we thought had done us wrong. We were to call them and do nothing but show our deepest and sincere appreciation for being who they were with zero expectations.

Zero expectations? Wow. This was no easy task. Most of us agreed that we were trained on some level to expect something in return when we give, consciously or not. And give when we're angry? It went against the grain. But the results were remarkable. Every attendee reported how deeply touched these people were when showered with appreciation. It's amazing how we desperately crave acknowledgement and appreciation from others but often forget to give it.

Several people in the workshop reported that family members and friends were concerned at first. Some broke down in tears. Some asked if they were dying! How amazing...we are so unused to appreciation that we're actually shocked when it happens. And how deeply healing it is to give thanks to another.

We often think of an interpersonal rift as impossible to cross over. Many of us have experienced, either first or second-hand, lifelong grudges where nothing seemed to help. It is awe-inspiring, the monumental difference gratitude can make in such situations. It can melt away years of anger and hurt feelings.

The Physical Benefits of Gratitude

Practicing gratitude is not just for the benefit of others. Research has shown that gratitude will make you happier and healthier. Biochemical changes happen when you are in a grateful state, as opposed to being depressed or angry. Your body reacts in a completely different way. And as a result, you will be better equipped to handle everyday stress.

According to Robert A. Emmons, Ph.D., in his pivotal book, *Thanks! How Practicing Gratitude Can Make You Happier*:

> *Our groundbreaking research shows that grateful people experience higher levels of positive emotions such as joy, enthusiasm, love, happiness, and optimism, and the practice of gratitude as a discipline protects a person from the destructive impulses of envy, resentment, greed, and bitterness. We have discovered that a person who experiences gratitude is able to cope more effectively with everyday stress, may show increased resilience in the face of trauma-induced stress, and may recover more quickly from illness and benefit from greater physical health.*

Other positive side effects of gratitude include: higher immune function/system response, expansive thinking and creative problem solving.

Though, of course, you can't be grateful simply for better health benefits. Gratitude must come from an authentic place in order to reap the rewards. Gratitude is always about the other. (And really, couldn't we all stand a break from focusing so much on ourselves?)

As Deborah Norville says in her book, *Thank You Power*:

> *Real gratitude is an others-focused emotion in which the emphasis is on the giver, not one's betterment or psychic improvement.*

Shift the focus from yourself onto the people around you. How can you add value to other's lives? As Albert Schweitzer says, "A person starts to live when he lives outside himself." You get the health benefits and so do others!

Women & Gratitude

As women, we're often harsh and critical of ourselves. (No surprise, right?) Well, that inner demon impacts all aspects of our lives, from intimate relationships to our performance at work. We seem to cling to a vision of perfection that is nearly impossible to achieve. When we don't attain it, we put ourselves (or others) down. It's only when we start appreciating ourselves "as is" that we can release that demon back into the wild and start celebrating who we are now.

Most of us have been taught to never toot our own horn, so instead of telling ourselves how wonderful we are, or at least congratulating ourselves for trying so hard, we look for faults instead, whether it be our weight, our age, our clothing, our status...the list goes on and on. Gratitude can be a way to gain back self-confidence. That nasty habit of vicious self-critiquing lessens and eventually disappears.

Breaking the habit of negative self-talk is not easy. Sometimes it can feel next to impossible. Why? Because it's deeply ingrained, especially for women who often seem programmed to dislike how they look, how they act and how they feel. And just like quitting any other nasty habit, it takes vigilance and time.

Start with the mirror (which is where our inner demon has a field day). Quietly note to yourself the ways in which you berate your appearance. Don't try to fight it. Allow it to be, notice it. Then simply add something you appreciate about the way you look, no matter how small. This addition will begin to shift your frame of mind and allow you to be more objective and less harsh. These small steps break that worn-out old record in our heads and allow for a new song to play.

Then move on to the outside world, where that inner demon preys on other people. Remember, we all encounter annoyances during an average day, but how we react is our choice. The next time that person cuts you off in traffic or jumps in front of you in line, take a moment for gratitude. *What*, you ask? *Gratitude? For people being rude?* Yes! You are given a challenge to practice inner peace in the face of adversity. Rise to it!

Is this easy? No. When you're genuinely angry, it can sometimes feel impossible. But every situation is made up of moments and each moment holds a potential for change. Most of the time, when we're angry, we react in a knee-jerk manner. The goal is to take a moment before that reaction; take a breath and a step back. Then look for anything, even the opportunity to rise above rudeness, for which to be grateful.

Once when a customer representative was impolite to me on the phone, I felt the urge to react negatively (to say the least). I found my voice rise as I tried to get my point across. As she continued to interrupt me, I took a moment—just a brief moment—to breathe and look out the window. The sun was setting and I was alive, arguing with another woman on the phone. It wasn't a perfect scene, that's for sure, but it certainly wasn't the worst. Interestingly, taking that moment to be quiet and check out the scenery de-escalated our situation and we were able to resolve the difficulty.

So as you can see, women often struggle with gratitude because of our embedded self-critical training. But with a little presence and patience, you'll begin to notice a difference. You'll see that glaring imperfection of yours as an interesting and unique feature. That annoying co-worker teaches you to stand up for yourself. As a woman who lives in gratitude, you begin to be at peace with yourself, then naturally, with others.

Gratitude for Our Loved Ones

Women are relational creatures. So a key opportunity to express and experience gratitude is with our loved ones. My husband and I actively practice gratitude with one another, even when times get tough. Sure, it's a challenge but the pay-offs are limitless. Gratitude becomes an endless source that we continually return to for support. This "practice" of ours has helped defuse arguments and keeps our love active, strong and ongoing.

We still have our challenges and push each other's buttons, but we never stay angry at each other for too long because we both choose to return to a state of gratitude, which is greater than the petty annoyances all couples experience.

The people in our lives are our teachers. We must be grateful for the lessons, no matter how hard. Again, it's not easy. It takes patience and awareness right before your knee-jerk reaction. Perhaps you have a friend that's consistently flaky, showing up late for events. As you're waiting in a lobby and your anger begins to rise, ask yourself what you like about this tardy friend. Maybe they have a fantastic, infectious laugh or hug you tightly, with meaning, just when you need it. You can still express frustration or disappointment for her lateness but this little bit of acknowledgement helps ease your rising blood pressure.

When you can focus on the love you feel for the other instead of the fears dancing around in your head, the tides begin to shift. That gentle mind shift, even during hard times, can make a huge and lasting difference.

Lessons in Gratitude

Pauline is good friend of mine and a generous soul who touched my heart in a profound way the minute I met her. She has a smile that radiates joy and gratitude. Her zest for life is contagious and whenever we spend time together, I feel rejuvenated and content. She just has that effect on people.

But life hasn't been easy for Pauline. Born with no arms and no legs, she's had to face challenges in life most can't imagine. But those challenges have also brought her blessings. Because of her disability, she relies on the unconditional goodness of others to help and support her. This has made her an extremely grateful person. She not only lives in gratitude, she teaches us to do the same:

> *I've had more opportunities than most to receive help, so I appreciate it more deeply because I can't necessarily reciprocate. People help me not because they are*

> *expecting anything from me but because of the pure kindness of their hearts. My life has given me the opportunities to receive that kind of help.*
>
> *On the other hand, for those giving the help, I think they also receive something in return. They receive the joy of experiencing themselves at service, without obligation or expectation. It's a beautiful dance that most people don't get the joy of having with other human beings, even strangers.*

One of the greatest lessons I've learned from Pauline is that gratitude can't be a byproduct of comparison:

> *I think I stir up gratitude when people see me because they occasionally say, "Wow, I'm so grateful for what I have because compared to you, my problems are nothing." But my deeper hope is that people don't find gratitude from a place of comparison or seeing others in a worse situation. I want people to see that they can be grateful for what they have, even in times of darkness.*

Gratitude is a habit we all can cultivate. Women who are habitually grateful like Pauline will always look for things to be thankful for, no matter how difficult their circumstances.

How Dale Carnegie Helped Me

For a long time, I believed that gratitude was either something you had or didn't have, like a green thumb. I didn't realize it was something that could be cultivated, practiced and mastered until I did it for myself.

It was 1999 and I had just started a wonderful job working for the Senior VP of an investment company in the entertainment industry. I was so excited to learn all about the industry and work with incredibly smart professionals. I had survived a horrible divorce, moved to a new state and was ready to start a brand new life. But things weren't going to go *that* smoothly.

There was somebody in the office who didn't like me. In fact, she despised me. You know that look that someone can shoot your way that threatens to take your very breath away? That's how she "greeted" me each day.

What could I have possibly done to make her so angry, I wondered? I gently started asking other coworkers about her and soon found out that she had always wanted my position. And although she had applied for it, I was the chosen one.

I felt a little guilty at first but there was nothing I could have done to prevent this situation. I decided to take matters into my own hands and find a way to win her over. (If I was going to spend eight hours a day working with her, I had better find a way to make things work.)

I started looking into tools that could help me and came across Dale Carnegie's famous book, *How to Make Friends and Influence People*. What a lifesaver! I started applying the principles taught, such as asking her questions and showing genuine interest in her life. And even if she didn't smile at me, I smiled at her.

Then I began to look for things in her that I appreciated and relayed them to her, whether it was a witty comment or a nice scarf. When she spoke, I made a concerted effort to listen to her as intently as possible. Soon, the woman who had been my nemesis was warming up to me.

What was the main point Carnegie taught in his book? You guessed it. Appreciation. Genuine concern and gratitude for the people around you.

Steps to Cultivating Gratitude

There are many paths and opportunities to cultivating gratitude. Here are some to get you started on your own journey. But be patient and consistent with this process. Remember, the critical voices in our heads took years to develop. Only by developing a daily practice do we begin to make real progress.

- ***Try bite-sized gratitude.*** Practicing gratitude may not come naturally, so being grateful for seemingly lesser things can be a good place to start. These small things could include your favorite song on the radio, an unexpected smile from a stranger, a delicious dessert or an old movie on a cozy, gray day.

- ***Generate gratitude by giving to others.*** When we show our appreciation for others, it comes back to us. It never fails. One of the biggest secrets of the Universe is that whatever we give to the world, we get back. It's so simple but so powerful. This is what the Law of Attraction is based upon. If we give anger and hatred to the world, that's what we'll get back. Conversely, when we show appreciation and love to others around us, a ripple effect occurs and we become surrounded by people who appreciate us.

- ***Don't just think gratitude, feel it in your body.*** Sometimes we say thank you, but we do so mindlessly. Just as we allow our negative thoughts to affect our bodies (we all know that tight, constricted feeling, right?), we need to make room for the feeling of gratitude in our bodies, not just our heads. An opening, an expansiveness happens. You may notice your breathing deepens, or perhaps your shoulders relax, or your chest feels open and receptive. In general, you feel more relaxed, at peace, when you're in a state of gratitude.

- ***If you can't be grateful, try acceptance or surrender.*** Gratitude doesn't always come easy. We can't bully it into existence. And as women, it's important to not slip into a new pattern of perfectionism in our search for gratitude.

  Let go of the need to get gratitude "right." If you're experiencing a situation that is deeply affecting you and you can't connect with gratitude, let everything go and focus on simply accepting what is. This exercise often provides our minds and bodies with a sense of relaxation and acceptance—that alone can free up space for gratitude in the future.

- ***Expect miracles.*** Once you make gratitude a regular part of your life, expect miracles. Miracles are not just occurrences when the angels ring bells and the impossible happens. It's when life presents itself in all its wonder and beauty. Giving birth is a miracle, breathing is a miracle, manifesting your thoughts (good and bad) is a miracle. What feels miraculous to you today? A sunrise? A bee collecting pollen? The pattern of a cloud? A powerful dream?

  Life becomes an adventure when you live each day with a child-like eagerness to experience miracles in your life. And if nothing particularly special happens that day, it might as well have, because the effects on your body and mind are just the same.

- ***Understand the difference between pain and suffering.*** Challenges are a part of life; we all experience them. That's how we grow. When we resist the challenges and try to make them go away, we suffer.

  Pain is a part of life; suffering is optional. We will be much better prepared to handle challenges in our life when we recognize the difficulty we face with some perspective. Suffering occurs when we lose perspective and internalize. It's that old "Why me?" trap.

  When we can step back from a painful situation and take a moment, even just one, to recognize any potential good that may come out of it, we lessen the chances of suffering.

- ***Use gratitude to change a negative frame of mind.*** This is a more advanced gratitude technique but consider it a challenge you *want* to meet. The next time you feel yourself sinking into a funk, try that gratitude mind shift. Do something different to break an old pattern. Call someone you love, look at a photo album chockfull of joyful moments, gaze into your loved one's eyes. Engage in any positive action that will break the negativity spiral.

- ***Start a gratitude journal***. Every night before going to bed, write down three things you are grateful for that day. It can be as simple as finding a parking space or eating the perfect peach. If you ever get stuck and are not sure what you are grateful for that day, ask yourself this question: What *could* I be grateful for?

- ***Be a grateful observer of nature.*** Go to a nearby park or even your backyard and take in all the magic and beauty of our planet. We live such hurried lives that we often forget to stop and smell the literal and proverbial roses. Being with nature is one of the easiest and quickest ways to bring us back to a state of gratitude.

- ***Send a thank you letter.*** Write a letter of thanks to someone in your life who was kind to you. Deliver it to him or her in person, if possible. This simple act can deepen relational bonds with loved ones and lift spirits.

Reflections on Gratitude

- What's your interpretation of gratitude?

- What are you most grateful for in your life?

- In what areas in your life are you lacking gratitude?

- What are you secretly or quietly grateful for?

- Who are the people who make a difference in your life? What are some ways you could show them your appreciation?

- Who do you love? Who loves you?

- What are the things that make a difference in your life? What makes your life easier?

- Was there a time in your life you felt more gratitude?

- Was there a moment in your life where you were overcome with gratitude? (Try to come up with 10. Write them down and look at your list often.)

My Insights

Write down any thoughts and feelings that might have come up for you while reading this chapter.

Go to www.PowerVirtues.com/Gratitude to continue your journey of *Cultivating Gratitude.*

Conclusion

By this point, you may be asking yourself, "These power virtues sound great but how can I possibly incorporate all that I've learned? There's too much on my plate already."

The beauty of these lessons lies less in "doing" and more in "being." In other words, it's not about making radical changes to your life but opening your awareness to the existing power of these virtues on a daily basis. So take this book off your "to do" list and put it on your "to be" list instead!

The lessons you've learned in this book can serve as an inspirational tool whenever you're feeling tired, stressed or overwhelmed. Consider it your personal talisman. In a moment of need, simply hold the book and close your eyes for a minute. Go to a deeper part of yourself and ask the Universe to show you whatever it is you need to read. Then open the book, trusting that the page you open to will be the exact page you need to see.

You can also center yourself, take a deep breath and ask yourself, "What feminine power virtue do I need in my life right now?" When you feel like you have received the answer, reread that chapter. As you do, ask yourself, "How does this apply to me now?" or "How can I access this virtue in my life?"

You can also head straight to the end of the chapter and re-work the suggested exercises. This will help you reconnect with that virtue and shift your energy to where it needs to be.

Using *The 5 Feminine Power Virtues* in Your Daily Life

The 5 Feminine Power Virtues are resources you can access at any time, whenever needed. The more you understand and practice them, the more readily accessible they are during a difficult period. Consider them a new set of spiritual tools in your personal toolbox. That's how I think of them—and I use them everyday.

The 5 Feminine Power Virtues in Action

Here's a personal example:

As I was writing this book about being feminine and powerful, I realized suddenly that I was allowing a rather insignificant event affect my state of being. Although I wasn't proud of my reaction, I also saw it as a wonderful opportunity to put into practice *The 5 Feminine Power Virtues* for my own growth.

I registered for a four-day health event that I had purchased tickets for two years earlier. It was costly to attend but I had heard great things about it and was excited.

Then some rumors began to mill about. The event used to include speakers like Deepak Chopra, John Gray and other talented individuals. Now apparently, they were just prerecorded videos of them. As the event neared, I heard about more services that were no longer being offered.

I still had hopes that it was going to be a great event but when I got to the registration table, I was informed that even more of the services previously offered had been cut from the program...or offered at an additional cost! But what really took me over the edge? Because I was not staying at their hotel, I was going to have to pay $45 per day to cover my meals (and we were doing a juice fast!).

I was so angry that I almost cancelled my reservation on the spot. If there were any way I could have asked for my money back, I would have. I felt completely cheated. *How could I be so stupid and let them take me for a fool?* I was losing control over my emotions very quickly.

Then I decided to take a "time out" and walked outside for a bit. I allowed silence to come over me. *I know better than this. Why is there so much anger inside of me? None of it is productive or constructive.* I just let all of the thoughts and feelings sit for a while. Then I opened myself up to the lesson in all of this. (There is always a lesson in every situation. The stronger your emotional reaction, the bigger the lesson.)

I thought of *The 5 Feminine Power Virtues* that I had been writing so fervently about. I asked myself which one could best serve me in this situation.

I started with presence. Did I need presence right now? I felt present. I also felt angry and in the moment. I might not be accepting of the moment, but I was in it, experiencing it.

How about authenticity? I felt authentic; it certainly wasn't the nicest side of me, but I was authentically experiencing anger and frustration...and then some.

Can spirituality help me? It was a challenge to feel spiritual when I felt angry at the world. Sensuality? Nope...had zero interest in feeling more sensual or in my body right now.

What about gratitude? Hmmm...now I was on to something.

I immediately started feeling more peaceful as I thought about everything I felt grateful for, such as how I found out about this program in the first place and how my life had completely changed after I discovered the people who organized it. I also took the time to acknowledge how all of their events in the past had made a huge impact in my life.

And then I remembered how the money I'd used to pay for the event had just showed up for me. I registered for the event after leaving the corporate world and had no idea how I was going to pay for it but I believed I was meant to attend it. My faith didn't let me down and four months later I received a substantial and unexpected refund from my income tax that covered the entire cost of the event.

Suddenly I realized there was no reason for me to be angry. My perspective shifted completely. I could make a decision from a sound, relaxed place instead. As I was able to release my anger, I created a space to have the most amazing four days at this life-changing event. But none of it would have been possible if I had stayed stuck in my negativity.

This practice of "scanning" *The 5 Feminine Power Virtues* has been part of my life ever since, no matter what life encounters I experience. And since my mind and spirit is so used to the process, I can often defuse difficult situations quickly.

Here are a few other spiritual resources you can use, in addition to the lessons learned in this book:

- ***Arrange time with a trusted friend or two*** so that whenever you are going through a challenge, you have each other for unconditional support.

- ***Find a community of women whom you feel connected to*** and either meet with them locally or chat with them online. Women need this connection with other women; it replenishes our souls. That's one of the reasons I created a free online community just for women who are on the path of self-empowerment.

  Make sure you join us at www.FeminineSoul.com. You'll have access to our groups and forums where visionary and empowering women collaborate and share their stories. You'll also receive our newsletter with inspirational tips and articles designed to connect you to your feminine essence.

- ***Focus on healing and nurturing your body.*** I can't emphasize this enough. When we take care of our body by feeding it the right foods, giving it proper exercise and being in touch with our feelings, we will feel much stronger physically, emotionally and spiritually.

- ***Get outdoors.*** There is nothing like nature to beeline you to your spiritual side. A simple walk or bike ride will bring you in touch with the greater powers of the Universe. Make time for it every day and take note of how differently you feel upon returning. Sit with this new feeling for a few minutes, in a state of gratitude.

On a Closing Note

You are a divine being. This is an ultimate truth. *The 5 Feminine Power Virtues* just brought you that much closer to your innate, brilliant divinity. Now the rest is up to you.

But remember, like any other learning process, it takes time, dedication and patience. Each day brings another opportunity to practice these new skills, honed from a place of self-love and empowerment.

Allow yourself to be confused or make mistakes. There is no right way to blaze your trail, only *your* way.

I'd like to end with one of my favorite inspirational messages:

"Our deepest fear is not that we are inadequate.
Our deepest fear is that we are powerful beyond measure.
It is our light, not our darkness, that most frightens us.
We ask ourselves,
Who am I to be brilliant, gorgeous, talented, fabulous?
Actually, who are you not to be?
You are a child of God.
Your playing small does not serve the world.
There is nothing enlightened about shrinking
so that other people won't feel insecure around you.
We are all meant to shine, as children do.
We were born to make manifest the glory of God that is within us.
It's not just in some of us; it's in everyone.
And as we let our own light shine,
we unconsciously give other people permission to do the same.
As we are liberated from our own fear,
our presence automatically liberates others."

- Marianne Williamson

Recommended Resources

Living *The 5 Feminine Power Virtues*
Continue your journey of exploring *The 5 Feminine Power Virtues* with videos, audios, events, and more. Go to:

www.PowerVirtues.com

Feminine Soul Community
Collaboration is key for women. The Feminine Soul community is a virtual home where women can connect and collaborate with other empowering and visionary women. Go to:

www.FeminineSoul.com

Feminine Soul Radio Show
Each week, Vanessa Halloum interviews women from around the world to discuss different methods to tap into our feminine power. For more information or to listen to previous shows:

www.blogtalkradio.com/FeminineSoul

Speaking Engagements
For more information about having Vanessa Halloum speak at your next event, send an email to info@vanessahalloum.com or call 504-5-DIVINE (504-534-8463).

Acknowledgements

First and foremost, I'd like to thank the following wonderful women in my life, who inspired me to write this book:

My mother Solange, for teaching me what it means to live with an open, feminine heart.

My sister Aline, for believing in me and teaching me my own strength.

My goddaughter Priscilla, for teaching me what it means to be a strong, feminine soul at such a young age and inspiring me to follow the path I'm on today.

My niece Erika, who lifts my heart with the sound of her contagious, innocent laugh.

My grandmother Vó Maria, for teaching me to believe in something bigger than myself and for having so much faith in me.

I'd also like to offer my heartfelt gratitude to:

God, my Creator, who is always by my side, guiding and inspiring me to help co-create a harmonious planet by bringing more balance between the divine masculine and feminine.

My female mentors and role models whose courage to step into their feminine power and change the world have continually inspired me: Marianne Williamson, Byron Katie, Princess Diana, Mother Theresa and many more.

My wonderful friends: Valeria, Angela, Bettina, Suzy and Ronit, for their love and support.

My writing coach, Laura Davis, for mentoring me and making sure this book was something I could be proud of and others would want to read.

My writing adviser and creative consultant, Beth Mann, for making my words and ideas sound so polished.

Thank you to all of my family, especially my father Jorge, for his love and support and for showing me the areas I have not yet mastered. To my brother Jorge, for his peaceful nature, which always inspires me to find my own center. And to my biological father Cicero, for inspiring me to explore my spirituality and inner wisdom.

And lastly, I want to thank the most important person in my life; the one that reminds me everyday of who I am and who I can become: my loving and supportive husband, Bassam Halloum. Without his love and support, I would never have followed my dream to write this book. Words cannot express how much love I possess for you and how deeply grateful I am to you.

Bibliography

Carnegie, Dale. *How to Win Friends and Influence People*. New York: Pocket Books, 1981.

Emmons, Robert. *Thanks: How the New Science of Gratitude Can Make You Happier*. New York: Houghton Mifflin, 2007.

Jarow, Rick. *The Yoga of Work*. Louisville, CO: Sounds True, Inc., 2005. Audiobook.

King, Theresa. *The Spiral Path: Explorations in Women's Spirituality*. Saint Paul, MN: Yes International Publishers, 1996.

Norville, Debra. *Thank You Power: Making the Science of Gratitude*. Nashville: Thomas Nelson, Inc., 2007.

Tolle, Eckhart. *A New Earth: Awakening to Your Life's Purpose*. New York: Penguin Group, 2005.

Vanzant, Iyanla. *Tapping the Power Within: A Path to Self-Empowerment for Women*. New York: Hay House, 2008.

Woodman, Marian. *Bone: Dying into Life*. New York: Penguin Group, 2000.

About The Author

Vanessa Halloum is an author, coach, speaker, seminar leader and the founder of *Feminine Soul*, an online community for women who want to connect and collaborate with other visionary women.

She's the host of the *Feminine Soul Radio Show* on Blog Talk Radio, where she has in-depth conversations with incredible women on how to live empowering and inspiring lives. Her mission is to help women reconnect with their feminine essence so they can access their inner authentic power.

She's also the President and CEO of Empowered Life Productions, a company dedicated to creating and marketing empowering products, programs and events that will make a positive impact in our world.

Originally from Brazil, Vanessa currently lives in South Florida with her loving husband, Bassam.

Meet Vanessa at www.VanessaHalloum.com.

CPSIA information can be obtained at www.ICGtesting.com
Printed in the USA
LVOW081404150512

281840LV00001B/12/P

9 780985 498306